Scar

Scar

a poem by

Carrie Etter

Shearsman Books

First published in the United Kingdom in 2016 by
Shearsman Books
50 Westons Hill Drive
Emersons Green
BRISTOL
BS16 7DF

Shearsman Books Ltd Registered Office
30–31 St. James Place, Mangotsfield, Bristol BS16 9JB
(this address not for correspondence)

www.shearsman.com

ISBN 978-1-84861-487-1

ACKNOWLEDGEMENTS
This poem was informed by the following works:
'Updating the Illinois Wildlife Action Plan: Using a
vulnerability assessment to inform conservation priorities';
Naomi Wolff's *This Changes Everything*;
The White House's 'Fact Sheet: What Climate Change Means
for Illinois and the Midwest,' dated 6 May 2014;
the Environmental Justice Climate Change report, 'Climate of Change:
African-Americans, Global Warming and Just Climate Policy';
a day with Rachel McCarthy at The Met Office;
and conversations and interviews with Illinoisans.

Special thanks to Susie Campbell and Claire Crowther
for their readings of, and responses to, the poem.

i.m. Peter Reading

at my beginning: prairie

at my beginning: a town called   Normal

on the far horizon   cornfield upon cornfield splayed

                      flattened by tornado

stunted stalks, palest soil under   a heavy sun

      soybeans   submerged in water

but no—   not far:

          today, tomorrow

so here's   The White House's "Fact Sheet:
                        What Climate Change Means

                                    for Illinois and the Midwest"

its list, its gist

            the volume's rising:

                        more heat
                        more pests
                        more disease
                        more extreme weather events:

                                    tornado
                                    drought
                                    flood
                                    heat wave
                                    blizzard

O Illinois—

more tornadoes

    one scours a half-mile-wide path through Fairdale

flattens / twists / hurls   homes / cars / a child's treehouse

    its scar in the earth visible

            from space

(off-page I am

    feline slink,

        butterfly shiver,

            fish glide, I am

                animal amid)

more tornadoes

and if you haven't a basement or cellar?

who hasn't a basement or cellar?

apartment-, trailer-home dwellers

yeah, you know

more heat waves

and in Chicago, amid concrete, asphalt   heat islands

    heat islands

    and who lives there?

(In Illinois, am I the cicada
    gnawing through summer nights,

the cow raising its gaze
    at the wind's shift,

the field mouse scrabbling
    in grain-rich dirt...)

more droughts

    in Illinois, a farmer crumbles
    earth between thumb and forefinger

    and in Egypt, a mother counts coins, reckons
    the cost of bread

more floods

    and the crops drown   go to mud

    "A year's amount of rain in a month
        and a half: 25 to 30 inches of rain," one farmer said.

    "It's a wonder we aren't all alcoholics."

(into air I become the awe of red   or yellow

    cardinal or goldfinch and

at times more modest

    house wren or sparrow

not even a quiver

    along the branch)

more blizzards

the descent quickens   thickens
less and less sky   tree   land
more and more white and the wind
a low whistle speeds into a whine
a quake in the panes
and now only an occasional flicker of color
amid the white throttling   the house

In the kitchen, the buzz of the CB radio.
He raises the microphone to his mouth:
Break 31 for Cindy Bear—
Cindy Bear, are you there?

I—nine? ten?—stand in the dining room's peripheral darkness
and watch him flick dials,
switch between the emergency channel
and our usual and back again.
My father grows smaller—
can one *grow*—yes, he grows—smaller,
he sweats, he calls again, he begs,
he says *she was going to Zayre's,* he says

(he doesn't say *hey hey hey this is Yogi Bear!*)

white shakes the glass and I realize
I'm holding my breath—

along the Mackinaw
                    plant trees and more trees

    to shade, to cool
                    smallmouth bass

                        southern redbelly, blacknose dace

and head northwest   to the sand prairies

    make them safe   and the ornate box turtle   thrives

now to find rocky outcrops   nurture oak openings

    for the slender glass lizard   timber rattlesnakes

and last *(never last)*   and here (*and here, and here*)

        the wetlands: common moorhens

            king rails   marsh wrens:

    so they live

The apologies shine like coins in the bowels of a fountain—

(and I burrow down

amid beetle and muskrat

woodchuck and snake

worm and rabbit

tunneling in the sure)

more tornadoes

sirens!
      and the children *s t r e a m*

        away from glass
             into, huddle against

    face the hallway's brick walls
    all those   primary colors
    so many   balls of skin and bone

every month, the children practice
    shield their bodies against
                    the possible

the apology song with its one shrill note—

more blizzards

      snow and more snow until the roads
        are no longer roads

      and a helicopter—with such snow, such winds—
        cannot deliver the heart

                  in time

(it's true: I bark and coo, swim and wriggle
flutter and slide, snort and screech

am animal amid animals—

and I annihilate.

I, the world's curse.)

www.ingramcontent.com/pod-product-compliance
Lightning Source LLC
Chambersburg PA
CBHW021950040426
42448CB00008B/1330